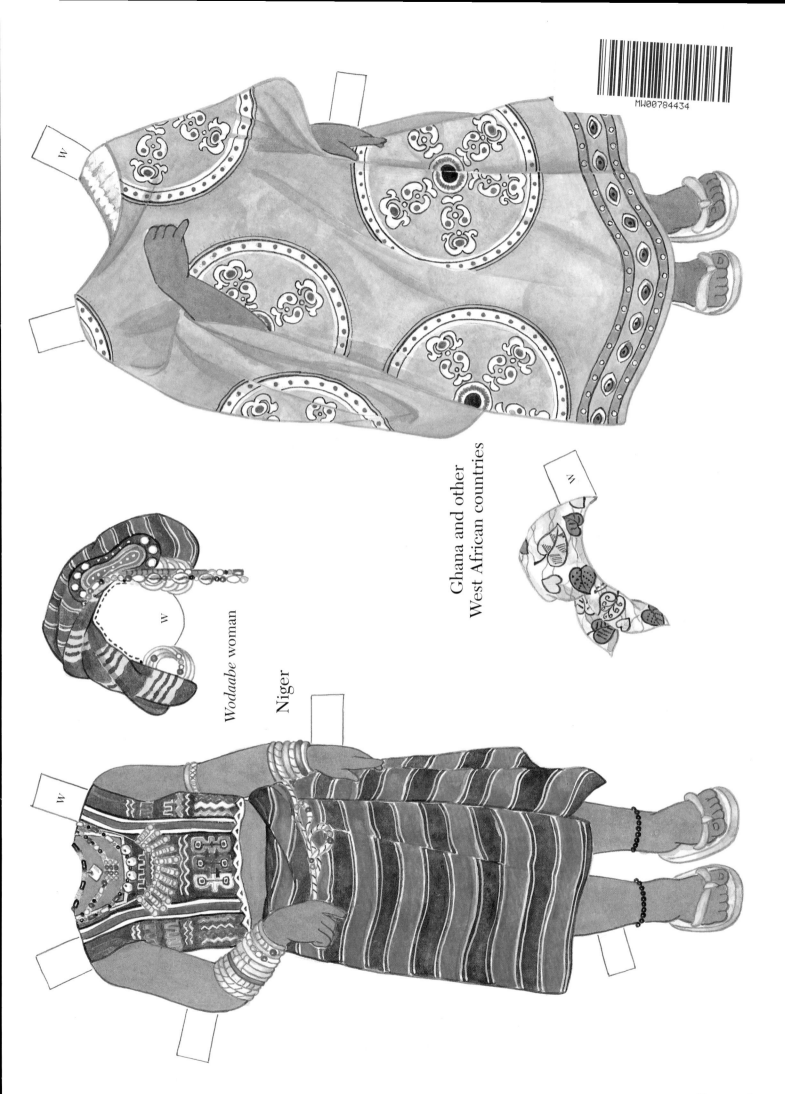

Wodaabe woman

Niger

Ghana and other
West African countries

PLATE 1

Ghana

Gold-plated state sword

Ceremonial gold-plated
headdress worn by chief

Ashanti man in *kente* cloth

Ashanti woman in *kente* cloth

PLATE 2

Ghana

Ga man with a
"Talking drum"

Ashanti woman
with a *kua ba* doll
(carved wood fertility doll)
in her waist

PLATE 3

Nigeria

Beaded hat

Ibo masquerade costume

Yoruba man in tunic with a "Talking drum"

PLATE 4

Nigeria

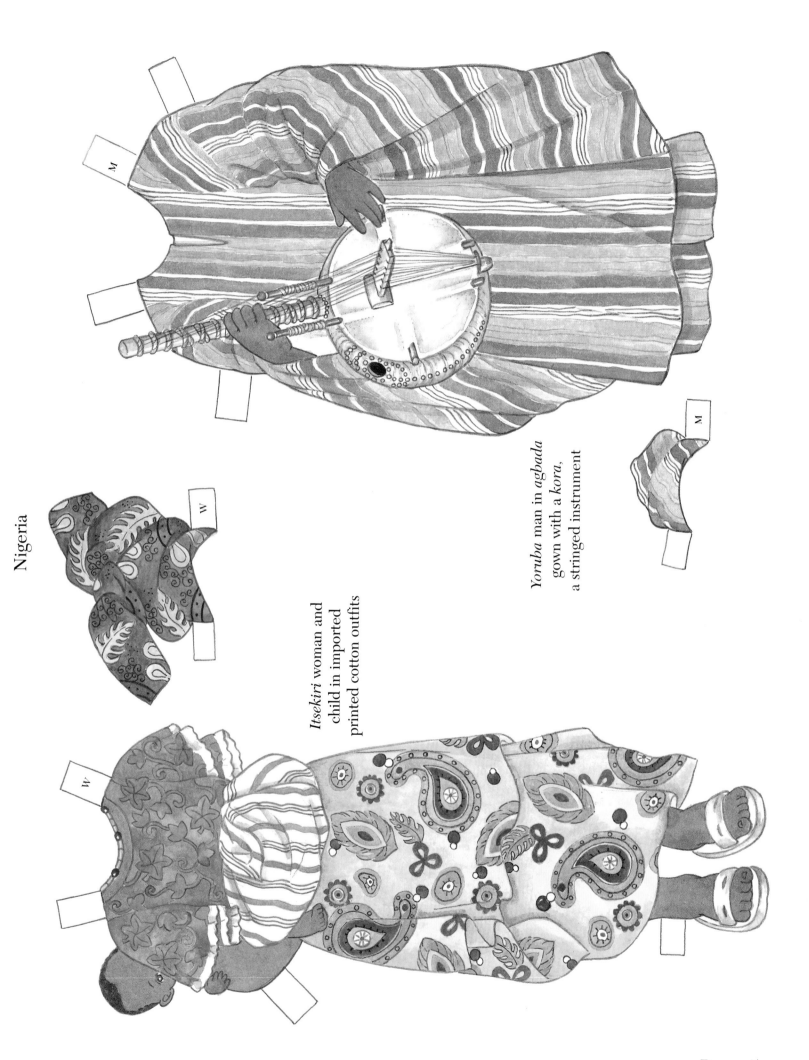

Yoruba man in *agbada* gown with a *kora*, a stringed instrument

Itsekiri woman and child in imported printed cotton outfits

PLATE 5

Kenya

slip tab behind head

Samburu woman and children (Nilotic)

PLATE 6

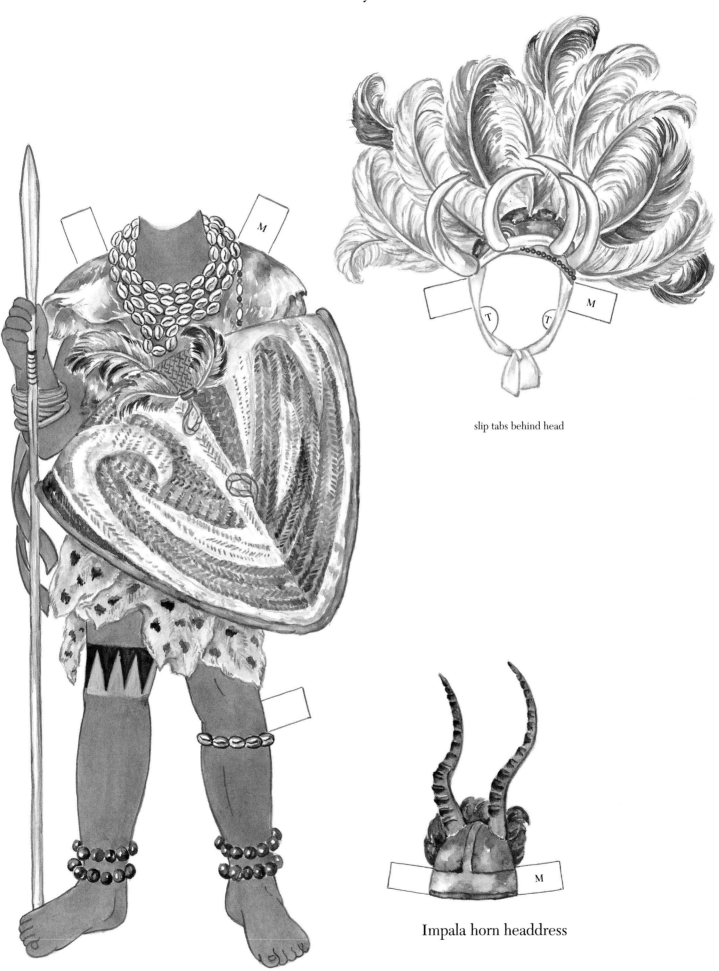

slip tabs behind head

Luo warrior (Nilotic)

Impala horn headdress

PLATE 7

Kenya

The ostrich plumers
(headdress)

slip tabs behind head

The lion's mane headdress

PLATE 8

Masai warrior in war regalia (Nilotic)

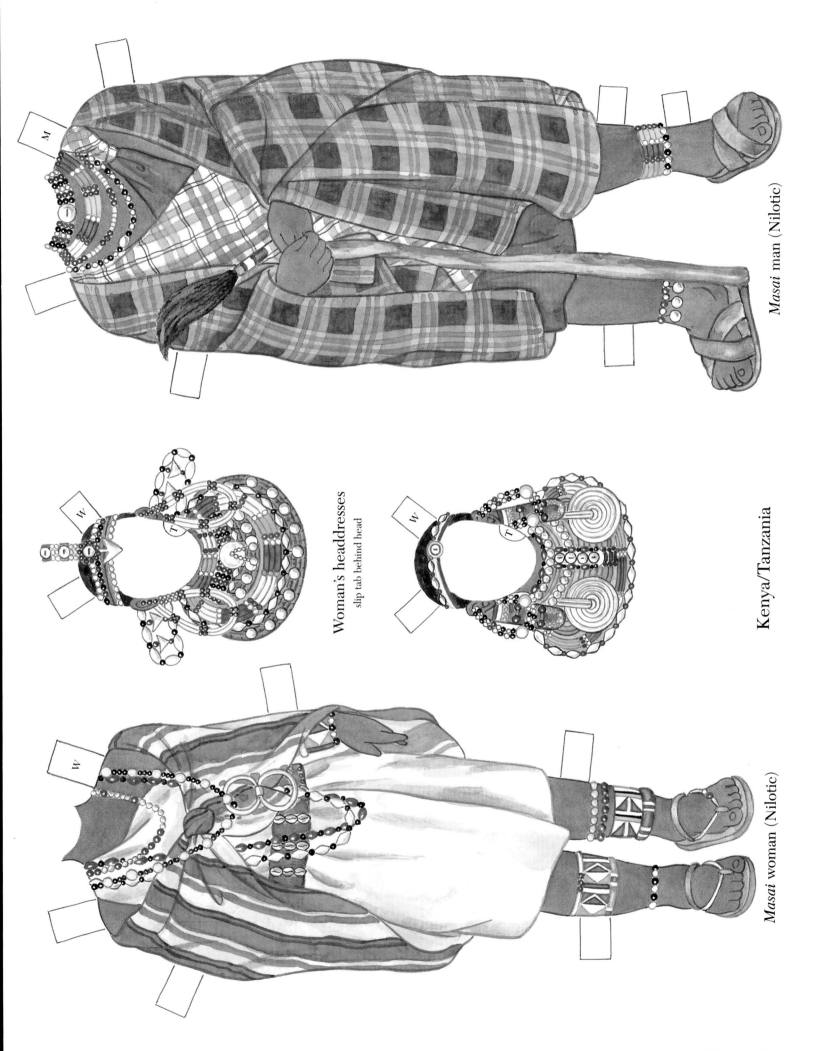

Masai man (Nilotic)

Woman's headdresses
slip tab behind head

Kenya/Tanzania

Masai woman (Nilotic)

PLATE 9

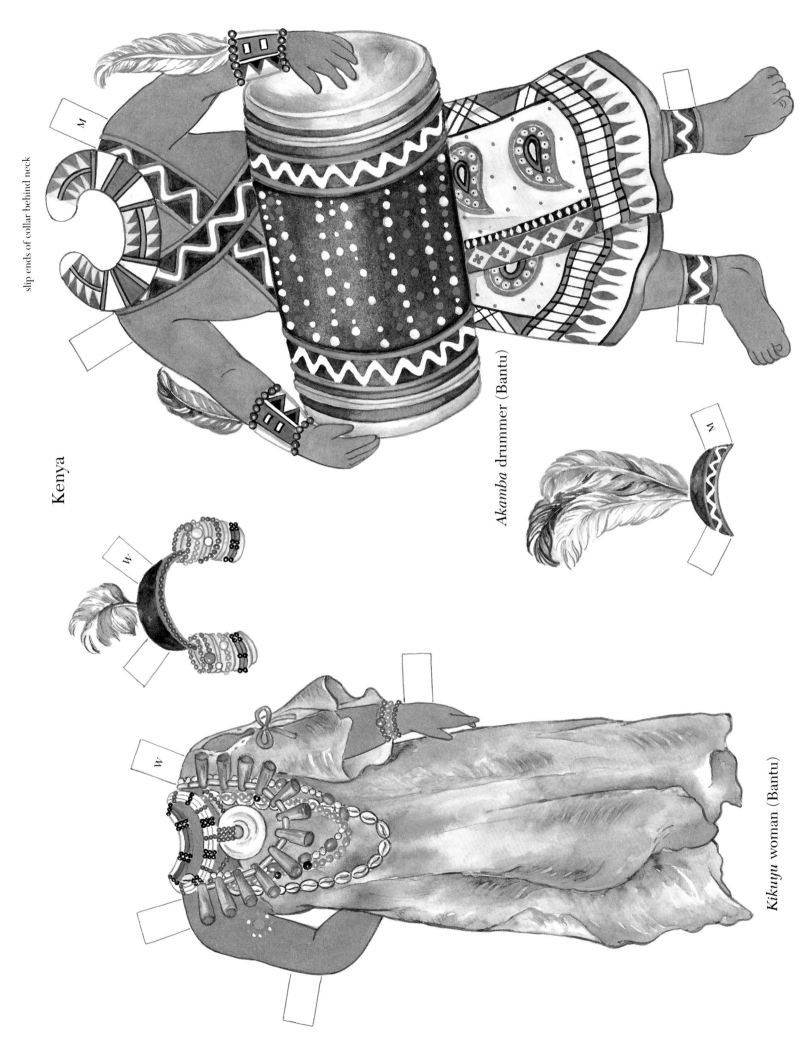

slip ends of collar behind neck

Kenya

Akamba drummer (Bantu)

Kikuyu woman (Bantu)

PLATE 10

Kenya

slip ends of collar behind neck

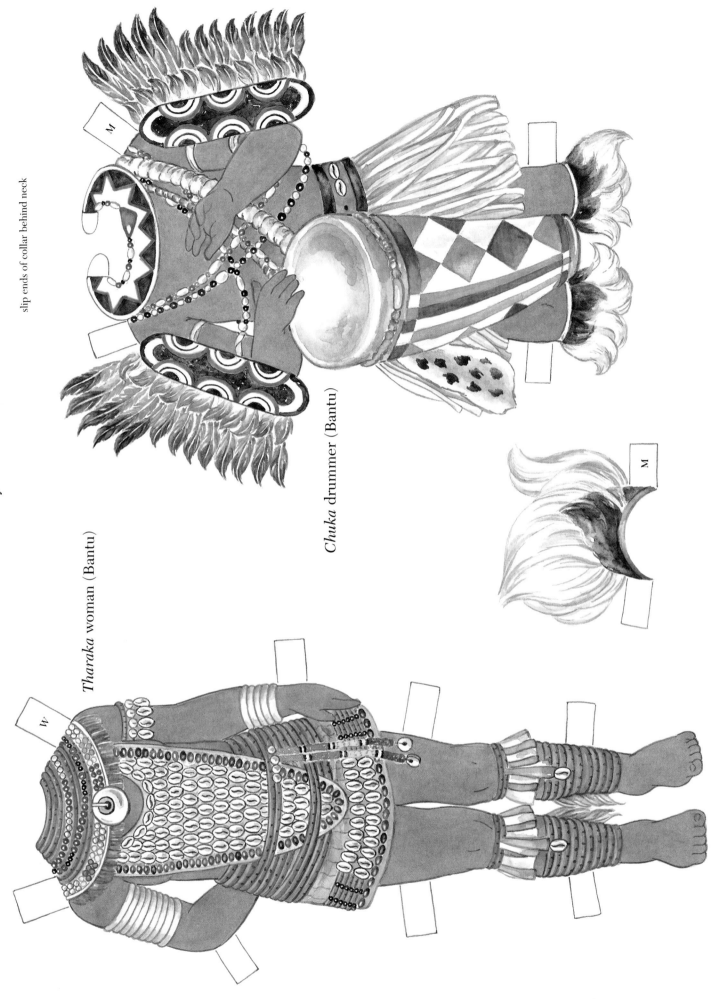

Tharaka woman (Bantu)

Chuka drummer (Bantu)

PLATE 11

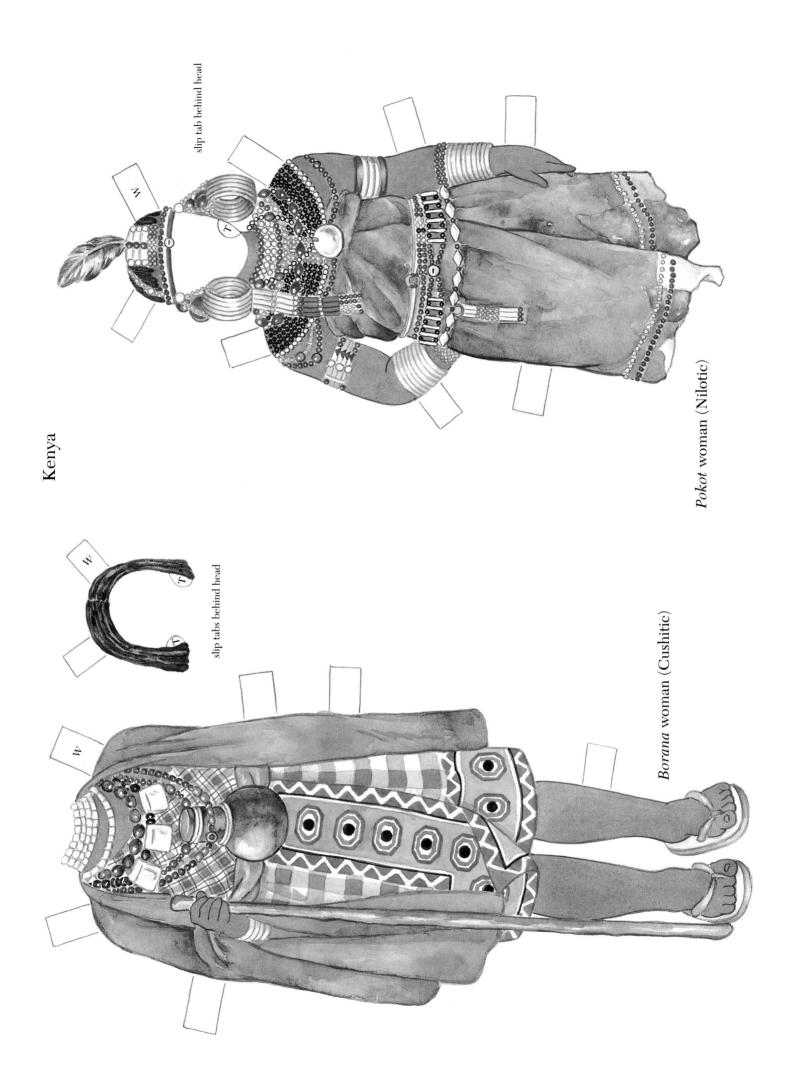

Kenya

slip tab behind head

W

T

slip tabs behind head

W

T

T

Pokot woman (Nilotic)

Borana woman (Cushitic)

PLATE 12

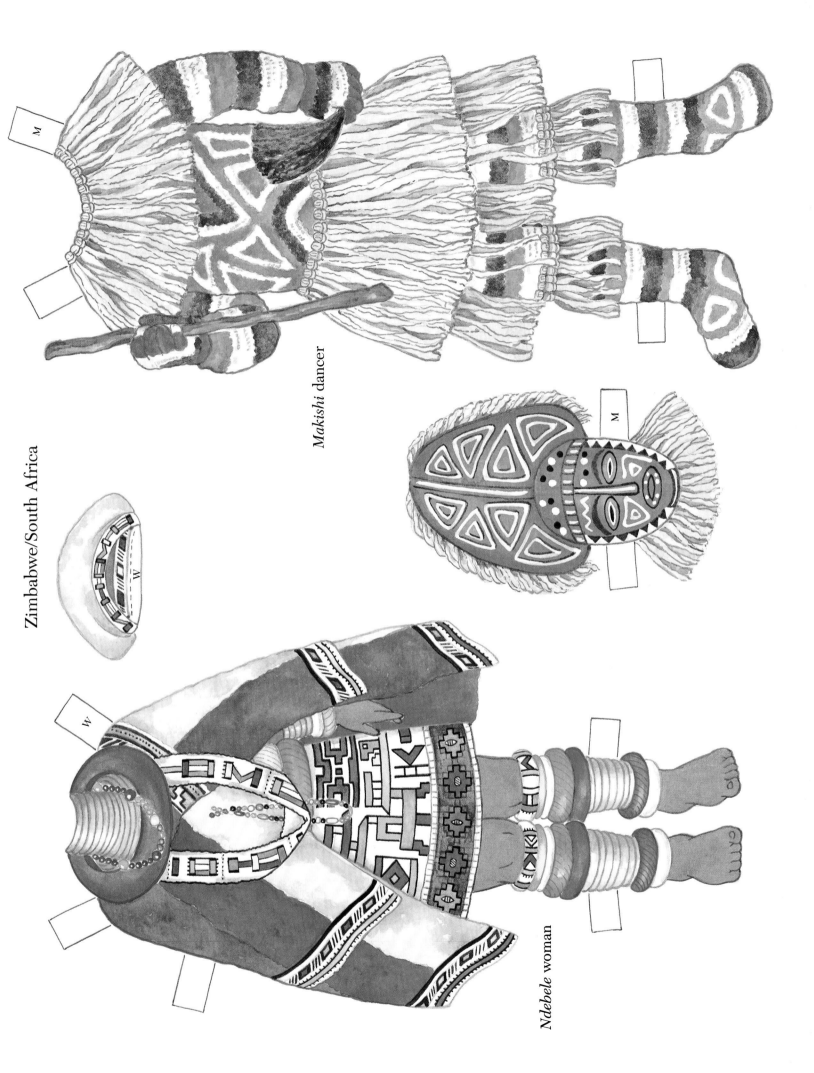

Zimbabwe/South Africa

Makishi dancer

Ndebele woman

PLATE 13

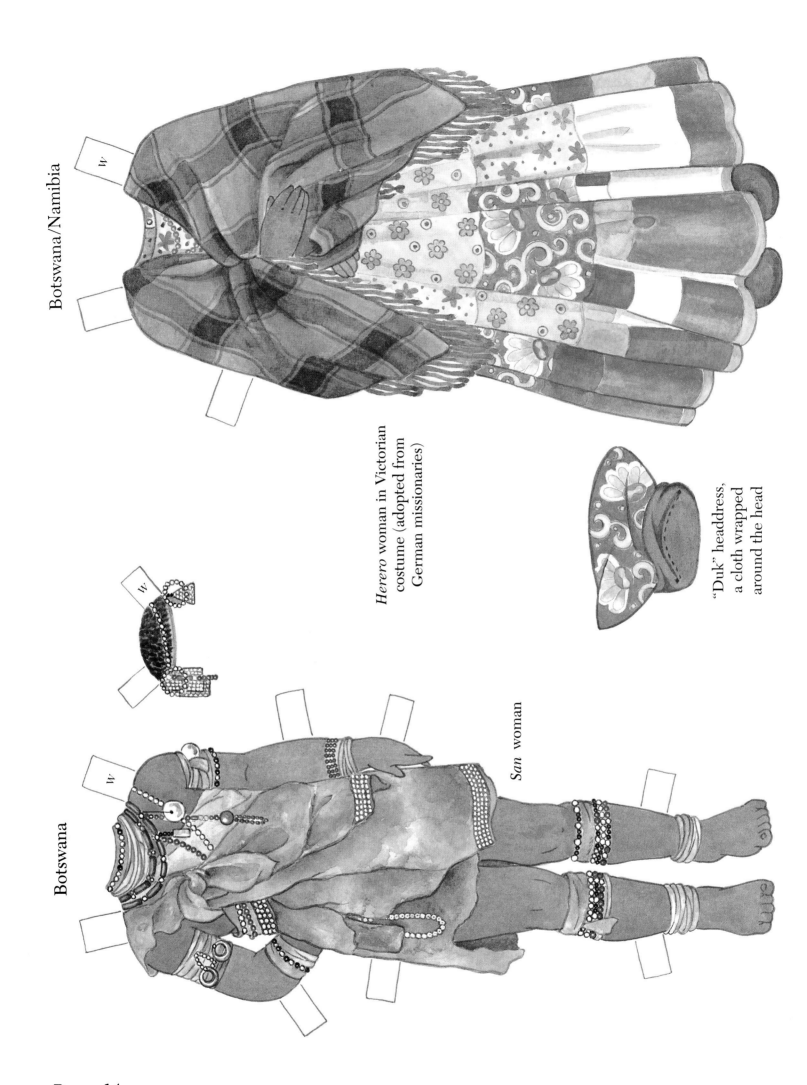

Botswana/Namibia

Herero woman in Victorian costume (adopted from German missionaries)

"Duk" headdress, a cloth wrapped around the head

Botswana

San woman

PLATE 14

Swaziland

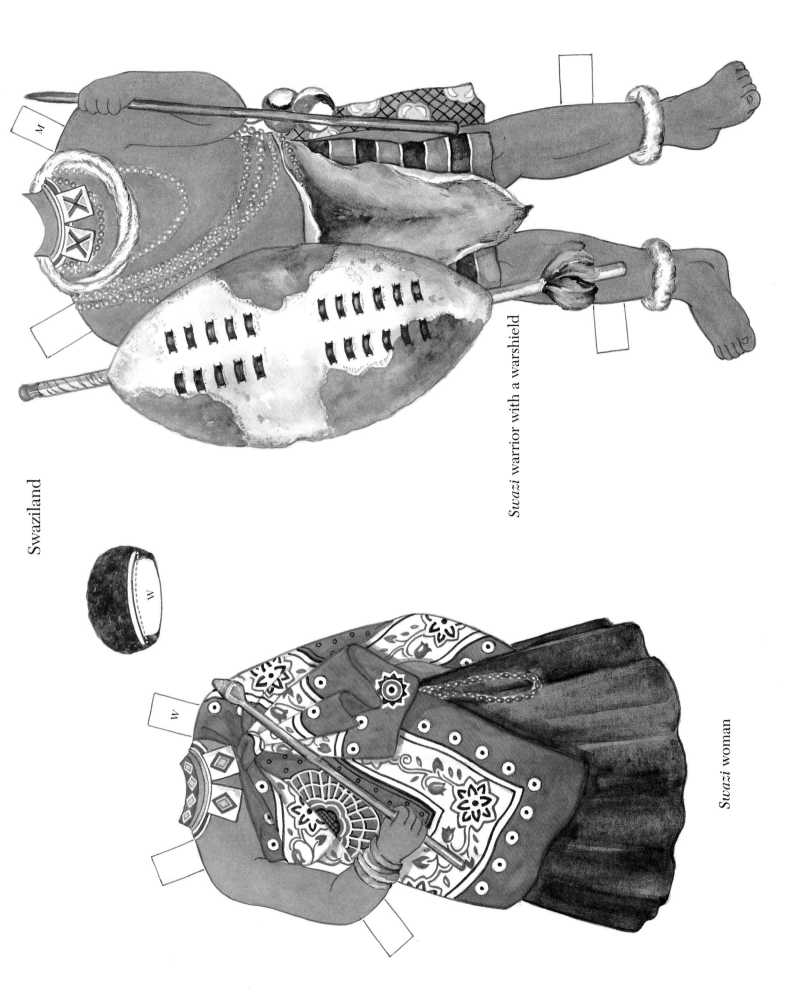

Swazi warrior with a warshield

Swazi woman

PLATE 15

Dyed ostrich headdress

South Africa

Zulu dancer with warshield

Zulu dancer